LEADERSHIP SECRETS

OF

"DEVIL ANSE" HATFIELD

12 Rules for Life, Horse-trading and Leading Folks

By

Charles K. Blankenship

ISBN 10: 149606772X
ISBN-13: 978-1496067722

FOREWORD

I was born and raised in Mingo County, West Virginia, the home of William Anderson "Devil Anse" Hatfield. His wife, Levicy (Levisa in some documents) Chafin Hatfield, was my maternal grandfather's (Julius Chafin's) aunt, and my paternal grandmother, Icy Pearl Blankenship, did household chores for Anse and Levicy in their declining years. The following is an apocryphal collection of letters from Anse to his sons - Joe, Cap and Tennis Hatfield, during those years at Stirrat, West Virginia (Logan County). I do not honor or glorify Anse. He was a notorious figure, remarkable for his conversion late in life. Given the popularity of the feud, it seemed a good vehicle to pass along these stories. Some long, some shorter, they contain tales told me by "Granny" Icy, leadership/deal-making principles I've gleaned from successful friends in nearly four decades in the coal business and some historical notes to provide context for the stories. I hope you enjoy them and take something from this book that you can use.

NOTE: The persons named above were real people and, while some liberties have been taken with timing and locations, they lived in Mingo and Logan Counties in West Virginia. Any person in this book seen in a pejorative light is a character who does not intentionally resemble any real person, living or dead.

My eternal thanks to my wife, Sue, who listened patiently to every story here and who encourages me when I need it, which is always. As well, thanks to my sons, Joe and Ben, who helped to edit this book and to Kyle, Patton and Lilly, who brighten my days.

>>TABLE OF CONTENTS<<<

William Anderson "Devil Anse" Hatfield

Hatfield ran a successful timbering operation in Mingo County as all of the activities of the feud were taking place. He knew how to lead men, in battle and on the job. In later years, he repented of his life of violence and was baptized. It is likely that he would want to be remembered for that act rather than as he is.

INTRODUCTION

Dear Sons:

It was good to hear about Joe's new job as Sheriff of Logan County, as well as Cap's and Tennis' jobs as deputies. Your Mother and I are very proud of you all. You have started on a path where you will be leading others and are responsible for how they perform. As you have heard, the doctor says I am not long for this world. This being the case, I want to pass on to you in writing what I've tried to teach in other ways. These are things I've learned in life, from my parents and from others, about leadership and just plain living. Hopefully, it will be a help to you. Right now, Vicie wants me to help with the goats, so I'll put this letter in the mail and send more as they come to me.

Love from your Dad,
William Anderson Hatfield

HISTORICAL NOTE : In his declining years after the feud ended, William Anderson Hatfield and his wife, Levicy, lived in a modest home in Stirrat, West Virginia on Island Creek. They are buried in nearby Sarah Ann in a hillside cemetery, and a statue marks the grave-site. Much has been made in recent years of the Hatfield-McCoy Feud, a collection of murders, shootings, stabbings and arson that spanned the years between 1863 and 1891, partially interrupted/fomented by the Civil War. It was a dark and bloody time, far darker than the various movies and stories produced to date. After 1891, "Devil Anse" Hatfield repented his sins and was baptized. His sons, Joe, Cap and Tennis, went from fugitives to law enforcement in Logan County, West Virginia in that same period. My maternal grandmother, Ada Blanche Browning Chafin, used to take food and drink out to her father's barn when Cap was hiding there from the law. Her father, "Red" Jesse Browning (so named because of the color of his hair), was a notorious bootlegger who was known to shelter fugitives from time to time. My grandmother said that she was very afraid of Cap, who had a bad reputation and who always spoke to her in a hateful tone of voice. Perhaps he changed in later years, or perhaps the people of Logan County were looking for that sort of man to impose order. Either way, she remained frightened of him.

CHAPTER 1

YOU JUST CAN'T HELP A LAZY MAN

Dear Sons:

As I write, I'm sitting on the ridge behind the home place and watching the fog thin out down in the holler. Doc Chafin (your Mother's kin) says it's good for me to get out and walk, so I've convinced your mother that it's okay for me to run the woods, too. She packed me a couple of biscuits with some goat cheese and a pint jar of buttermilk in a lard pail and asked me to bring back some huckleberries. So, I'm up here where they grow and enjoying the warm sunshine.

Joe, you were telling me in your last letter about your concern that some of your deputies seem lazy. If that's the case and they are truly a sorry bunch, you may as well start fresh with some new men and let those ones go. On the other hand, maybe they've just gotten into bad habits which can be changed if you line up their self-interest with yours. The way to do that is just to tell them how you want the job done and then explain that either they or their successors will get it done that way, but you want to give them first chance at it. Then, fire the first one you catch sloughing off. It's amazing what knowing that you are willing to pull the trigger will do for the men who just haven't been motivated up until now. Many a man thought to be lazy has stepped a little faster when bullets, instead of just threats, start to fly.

If they are lazy to the bone, cleaning house may be your only solution. I recall the story of a man over in Thacker, WV who was so lazy it hurt just to look at him. He had about a dozen children, and his wife worked as hard as she could – raising a garden, taking in washing and such when she wasn't rearin' a young'un, but he wouldn't strike a lick at a snake if it was gonna bite him. He was just no account.

Many's the time the local churches took up collections to help feed or clothe his family and, finally, his neighbors just got tired of sending food, clothing or cash to that house while he enjoyed his slothfulness.

Late one afternoon, about ten of them rode up to the house, snatched him out of the hammock where he was watching the world go by, hawg-tied him and threw him in the back of a wagon. Their intent was to take him up the holler and hang him, figuring that the family would need less help with one less mouth at the table.

As the men of the community approached the big oak where they intended to do the deed, they met the pastor of the Freewill Baptist Church. He was driving a wagon as well, returning from a visit with a church member. That man had given the pastor a load of field corn which could be ground for meal for the winter. The pastor pulled to a halt and asked the men where they were going with their captive. They replied that, since the lazy lout didn't have an asset to his name, they were just going to hang him and put the family out of its misery. The pastor then pleaded for the fellow's life and asked if they'd let him live if the pastor gave the man the wagon-load of corn. After some hem-hawing and sheepish looks, the men allowed that they would spare the sluggard over such a generous act.

At this, the bound man rose up to a sitting position in the wagon and asked the pastor in a loud voice, "IS THE CORN SHELLED?" When the pastor said "well, no, it's not even shucked", the condemned man lay back down in the wagon and called "DRIVE ON, BOYS!" So, you see, it's impossible to help someone who is truly lazy.

Well, I've been watching that empty lard pail for a while now, and it's not getting filled. Guess I'd better get to huckleberry picking before Vicie decides to get her a new picker. I'll get this in the mail tomorrow and, hopefully, have a nice piece of berry pie.

Love from your Dad,
William Anderson Hatfield

BUSINESS PRINCIPLE : After giving your people achievable goals, clear instructions and the resources to get the job done, they will fall into three categories – 1) people who are self-starters, who get the job done right the first time; 2) people who need a little motivation, but are otherwise able to reach the goal and 3) people who will never perform unless you are watching their every move. You need to reward and groom the self-starters for bigger things, reward and praise the ones who needed only a little motivation and CULL the rest. No matter how much it costs to recruit and train new people, those who only perform under duress will chew up too much of your time and energy to make it worth keeping them. You are doing yourself AND them a dis-service to keep them when they don't fit. The shock of being discharged may be what it takes for them to do better in their next job.

In my career, I have been responsible for leading people who fell into the three categories listed above. Thankfully, the majority were self-starters, who only needed to know which hill to take. I will always remember these folks fondly, and would still do anything I could for them. The people who needed a little motivation were never hard to lead and frequently surprised me when they produced better results than expected. Quite a few started out in this second class, then caught fire to become great self-starters. The non-performers I can count on the fingers of both hands. Most had the idea that they were somehow entitled to a paycheck and that they were players in a game to see how little they could contribute and still stay employed. I never fired any of these; they fired themselves. We made the expectations known, gave them every opportunity to produce desired results and then just handled the paperwork as they essentially decided to quit. While I have agonized over having to let some people go (during re-organizations, down-sizings, etc.), I've never lost any sleep when someone decided that they were going to refuse to work. There's an old joke where an executive is asked how many people work for him/her and that person responds with "about half of them". I am blessed to be able to say that my answer would be "the overwhelming majority of them".

HISTORICAL NOTE : There was no real safety net at the turn of the 20th century for people who couldn't or wouldn't work. They were supported (or not) by family members or by members of churches who were trying to extend a hand to the helpless. In some cases, there was the County Work House, where one could at least survive. There were then, as there will always be, some people who are unwilling to take up honest work to support their families. As now, those people depend upon what they can steal or get "under-the-table" to supplement whatever help comes from government, family or church connections. If those people put half the energy into an honest days' work as they do trying to beat the system, they would have plenty. Christ said "the poor you will have with you always", but could also have said that we will always have the lazy with us as well. This story comes from a time when doctors and ministers were paid with the produce from farms or firewood cut from the hills. While I have no documentation of any such hanging as this one, it is not too much of a stretch of the imagination to picture the one outlined above.

CHAPTER TWO

DON'T PLOW WHAT YOU CAN'T HOE

Dear Sons:

The old rocker on the back porch looked so good, I couldn't help sitting hyar a spell, and so decided to answer your letter before hoeing out the rest of the corn patch. I don't know what made me think in April that I'd be able to handle such a large garden in July, but it appears my eyes were bigger than my hands on this one. It puts me to mind of the plans Joe wrote about and the ideas for bringing change to Logan County. They are all good plans and ideas, you just need to decide how you're going to go about it. When you organize the things you want to accomplish into jobs you can do now, jobs that can be done within a few years (with help) and jobs that might take much longer, you can focus your energy on what is truly important. You will recall that I've always told you that when you shoot at a whole herd of deer, you will get no deer at all, but aiming at just one of them puts meat on the table. It's the same thing with the chores of life. If you try to be and do everything at once, you'll wind up worn out, with no results to show.

Years ago, old man Jake Harmon inherited some money from an uncle over in Richmond and commenced to buying up bottom land all over the county. He already owned a good team of mules and told me one day that he was fixin' to make himself a rich man by raising hundreds of acres of corn and sorghum he could sell in Charleston. Trouble was, Jake was stingy by nature, and no one would work for him for what little he was willing to pay for farm help. But Jake was more stubborn than he was stingy, so he took his team of mules and plowed every square foot of land he owned, including his own yard. He then took the last of his inheritance and bought seed, which he managed to get planted. The weather was good, and most of what he planted just popped right out of the ground. Jake was proud of his work and rode one of the mules from plot to plot, bragging to everyone he met about how well the crop was coming. But then came the time for hoeing and weeding. He was able to plow between rows to turn up fresh dirt, but found that hoeing and weeding took all the energy he had, and more. They found him one hot afternoon, lying on his back in one of his fields, with a hoe in one hand and the other hand grabbing a-holt of his overalls just over his heart. The old mule was standing in the shade down by the creek.

Old Jake died with no heirs, so the county eventually sold off all he owned for taxes. If he had been a little less cheap or less ambitious, he might've made out just fine. However, he was neither, and was generally mourned by no one. A sad way to go.

Well, the weeds are growing so fast this summer that, if I don't get the corn patch finished, it'll be time to start it all over again. Your mother and I dearly love sweet corn, even if we have to cut it off the cob nowadays. If you get a chance to come by in the next week or so, we'll load you down with a couple of bushels. What you don't eat fresh, you can pickle. I'd better get after it now and put this letter in the mailbox.

Love from your Dad,
William Anderson Hatfield.

BUSINESS PRINCIPLE: It is not uncommon in today's business community to see a company launch an acquisition program and, during its course, forget that they need to operate what they're buying and to do so at a profit. CEO's and Boards of Directors get so excited about cornering the market on their products or services that they paint themselves into that corner. A wise business leader will have a buy-assimilate-succeed cycle built into the M&A strategy. Those who lose their heads in the fog of acquisition will join the ranks of the sadder-but-wiser who have run their corporations aground. Know how you will pay for today's acquisition before you start working on tomorrow's.

I have seen first-hand what being an excited buyer and a burdened operator can do to a corporation. I worked for a company once who named a business model after itself which consisted of buying a small-

to-middle-sized, low debt company, running that company into debt as far as the lenders would allow and then using those funds to buy the next target. The previously low debt company was then left to service all of that debt AND to deliver handsome returns on its new owners' investment. When the folks who had been managing the smaller company before the takeover had tapped every possible one-time revenue source and proved unable to "print money" indefinitely, they were replaced with people who said they could, with mediocre results. That is not the way to run a successful acquisition program, because "buying" can't continue forever and "operating" has to start sometime.

In another case, a company decided it could reap great returns by buying up a lot of similar "mom-and-pop" companies and use economies of scale to provide overhead services to all of the small businesses. The buying company was so excited by the concept that it compensated its acquisition team on the volume of deals completed and not on the quality of those deals. This resulted in inadequate "due diligence" work which, in turn, resulted in the acquisition of millions of dollars in liabilities which were not immediately apparent. It seems that regulators of various stripes, in various states, will give more latitude when "mom-and-pop" have a serious problem than when Big Corp, Inc. has the same issue. The deal-makers did well for themselves, the small businesses got spun off to people who knew how to run them, and the buying company was lucky to get out with only the loss of a few hundred million dollars.

The coal industry has some excellent bad examples for your consideration. Over the last decade, there have been a number of acquisition programs which ran aground because buying took precedence over operating. More than a couple have found themselves with poor coal reserves that were being managed by very good people. Rather than incorporating the best practices and best people of those good operators into the buying company's management team, the buyer allowed those good people to leave for other jobs. This created situations where average coal operators were expected to pay for big acquisition costs with coal produced from poor-to-average reserves. Other coal company acquisitions have failed to look closely enough at safety and maintenance records only to find the buyers paying too much for a company which cut corners on both. If you will think about acquisitions carefully, you will find a way to make only those purchases which strengthen your company's position in your chosen industry. Being excited about gaining market share or just being bigger can easily lead to regret and, often, to the end of your career.

HISTORICAL NOTE : There is not a great deal of flat land in southern West Virginia. Most of it today is occupied by buildings, public and private. In the early 20th century, folks worked in the mines, on the railroad or in timber businesses (cutting or at sawmills) AND farmed what land they owned in order to feed their families. This was, for the most part, subsistence farming, where the family mule was used to plow the fields and everyone in the family who could work pitched in to keep the crops weeded, hoed, fertilized (courtesy of the mule and whatever other pigs, chickens or cattle they owned) and harvested. During the great Depression, the subsistence farmer would go into the woods, find gently sloping patches of land ("flats"), cut trees and brush from those areas and then plant corn or beans in those "hollow" fields. My mother reports seeing her father work all day in the mines and then hoe corn at night by his carbide light.

CHAPTER 3

A GOOD DEAL WILL WAIT FOR YOU

Dear Sons:

I noted, Joe, from your last letter, that a number of courthouse folks are shining up to you and trying to get you to throw in with them on first one issue or deal or another. That's to be expected, now that you are the sheriff. On t'other hand, it's also to be expected that not all of those people wish you well or want you to succeed in any form or fashion. I would caution you to be very careful when something appears to be a good deal. Most things that appear to be too good to be true just aren't true at all. What's dangerous about that is that it's all too easy to talk yourself into seeing what you want to see instead of what really is. You and I have seen too many coon-hounds barking up an empty tree to believe someone just because he appears fervent.

Vicie and me just got home from a wedding down at the church-house. Young Floyd Estepp is now married to Bill Dalton's girl, Molly, and they make a fine couple. She got a hard-working, sober man who will spend his life to make her happy. He got a girl who knows how to do just about anything around a farm (since she followed her daddy around all through her childhood, learning from him), who loves Floyd with all her heart and who is easy to look at. (Vicie says I shouldn't be worrying about that, but it's the truth.) I'm glad it all turned out well, especially given the doubts that some of us had along the way. You see, they were engaged for seven years while Young Floyd saved money to buy some land and build a cabin. Molly had other offers during that time, but she waited for the man she loved. Good deals are like that, if they're good today, they'll most likely be good tomorrow.

On the other hand, bad deals often have a short fuse. I recall the time when Isaac Kinder was looking for some timber land, with the idea of running up a sawmill and producing rough lumber. He ran into Lee

Varney down at the courthouse and, during the course of a conversation, Isaac learned that Lee had just inherited about 1,000 acres of prime timber over on Beech Creek AND that Lee was in a hurry to sell it. Well, they both rode over to Beech Creek to see the land and Varney gave Kinder a price, with the provision that the buyer would receive a 40% discount if the seller could get his money within 3 days. Kinder was happy with the deal, but knew that, this being Friday afternoon and Monday being a holiday, the courthouse would not be open until Tuesday. That meant that Varney couldn't give him a proper deed before the money had changed hands. Still, it WAS a good deal, and Varney offered him a quit-claim deed. The long and short of it was that Isaac gave Lee the money and Lee gave Isaac a piece of paper saying that, whatever rights Lee had to the property, he was giving them to Isaac. Come Tuesday, Isaac Kinder went to the courthouse to file the paperwork, only to find that neither Lee Varney nor anyone in his family had ever owned the timber on that land. Lee had the money and a three day head start. Isaac learned the hard way that you can move too fast in business for your own good.

That's about it for now. I need to feed the chickens and see if they've left us any eggs today. Be careful, and remember that we love you.

Love from your Dad,
William Anderson Hatfield

BUSINESS PRINCIPLE : Often in business, the best deal is the one you did not do. Negotiators who are in a hurry to reach an agreement can be their own worst enemies. It is amazing how many deals (purchases, acquisitions, labor agreements, etc.) should never have been completed in the form they were. There is a tremendous amount of "good will" sitting on balance sheets today because someone was in a hurry. If you are not being given enough time to carry out due diligence for a purchase, or to examine the details of an offer you are receiving, then you need to be prepared to walk away from the table. Consider that the reason the other party is in such a hurry is not in your best interest.

Speeding up the pace – in a race, a basketball game or a boxing match – is a common tactic to get one opponent stretched beyond his/her capabilities. Remember that a good deal will wait long enough to verify that it IS a good deal. As an old friend once told me, "Never get excited when you are buying".

Being as contrary as I usually am, I enjoy having someone call me at home with the "deal of a lifetime", a product or service that is so good that I'm losing money because the salesperson is required by law or an employer to take so long to explain it. Terms like "up to 30% return on your money within weeks" or "your good friend, Bill (or Bob or Roy), got in on this deal and wanted you to have the opportunity to take advantage of it as well". At this point, I will ask for a prospectus or at least a written summary of this wonderful offer and tell the caller that my wife and I will take a look at it and get back to him/her in a couple of days. The typical response is that information can be e-mailed to me, but that the offer is only available for the next hour (or two or three). Of course, that means I'm NOT interested, but it is often amusing (depending on how polished the seller sounds) to ask a number of questions about things like "typical returns", references I can call, etc. Now, if it is just a "kid" who is reading from script and who may suffer for my game, I will just say "No" and move on. If, however, it seems to be someone who has made a career of fleecing people, I don't mind dragging the call out a bit. As I said, contrary.

HISTORICAL NOTE : Buying property (timber, coal reserves, gas rights, etc.) in southern West Virginia is still tricky 100 years after the story above. Instead of the sensible property boundaries common in the Midwest, where the land is divided into sections and well-surveyed, many parcels of land in the hills have convoluted property descriptions. A deed may call for "from a tack in a chestnut stump up the hill for 75 rods to a stake on the ridge in the midst of three paw-paw trees, thence with the ridge-line for 250 rods and 1 link to an "X" scratched into a sandstone outcropping at the head of Sandy Fork of Pigeon Creek and thence down Sandy Fork and onwards with the northern bank of Pigeon

Creek 450 rods and one chain to the place of beginning". Given rotting stumps, forest fires, erosion of outcroppings and meandering of streams, it's hard not to feel sorry for the surveyor, much less the buyer.

Keep in mind that one may own a parcel of land "in fee simple", meaning that you own the land and everything on or under it or you may own surface rights, timber rights, grazing rights, mineral rights (to one, several or all of the minerals), natural gas rights (to one or several gas horizons) and/or oil rights. This means that, even in the best of circumstances, it may be hard to figure out what is owned by whom. Now, throw in issues of heirship, where one heir may own seven thirty-seconds of any or all of the above, and the plot begins to thicken. There are some properties in southern West Virginia where the heirs cannot agree on how such lands can be used or sold. The result is an old house and barn falling in on themselves in the midst of a patch of land reverting to forest. All of these considerations make title search companies worth their weight in gold.

Having said all of this, there are still people out there who will try to sell rights they don't own to people who are in too big of a hurry to figure out that the deal is a trap. "Caveat Emptor" is as applicable today as it was when the Romans ruled their empire.

CHAPTER 4

YOU CAN'T DO A GOOD DEAL WITH BAD PEOPLE

Dear Sons:

Before I go further, know for sure that dealing with good people won't guarantee a good deal. Sometimes a swap or a sale will look good to both sides, but one or both of you may lose something no matter how hard you both try. That's just a fact of life. Stand up straight, and get on with things. In the long haul, you'll both come out ahead by fair dealing. Trying to do business with a crooked man is another story.

You can't do business with a bad person and break even, let alone expect to come out ahead. If you try to be good to him, he'll take everything you give and ask for more. If you try to hold him to a deal, he'll try every trick in the book to get the upper hand. If you back him into a corner, he'll try to hurt you. When all is said and done, He'll either laugh at you behind your back or try to give you a bad name (or both). A little story will show you what I mean:

When I was about 10 years old, my Paw bought two coon-hounds. One was a redbone that came from Elias Cline, who lived down on Cow Creek, and the other was a blue-tick from "Uncle" Jopie Maynard, who lived over on Little Thacker Branch. Now, both dogs were good-looking animals, and their owners ran big packs of hounds that treed lots of coons. However, there was a lot he didn't know about the dogs, so he took them on a two-week trial.

On the first night of the trial, Old Blue (the dog from Little Thacker) struck a deer track about 20 minutes after Paw and I turned him loose. He hit the ridge about 15 minutes later and was long gone. We listened for about an hour before he went completely out of earshot down Horsepen Creek. He came back in at Uncle Jopie's place the next day, and anybody could see from the condition of his feet that he had been running deer. Uncle Jopie immediately saddled a horse and brought our money back, apologizing for the dog's fault. That's just the kind of man that Jopie Maynard was, and it was why people weren't afraid to trade with him.

That red dog (they called him Rattler) was another matter altogether. On the first night of his trial, we turned him loose behind the barn and had to walk around him all night. Honestly, that dog wet down every bush and tall weed he passed and never got out of our sight. Paw thought that Rattler just wasn't used to us, so we took him out every night for the whole two weeks. He never got more than 25 feet from us for the whole time! Then, we returned him.

When we drove into Elias Cline's yard on Cow Creek, I had never seen anything like it before. His house looked worse than our chicken coop and there were runny-nosed children and hounds everywhere. There was so much filth that Maw wouldn't let me get off the wagon. Paw took Rattler and knocked on the door. At first, Miz Cline said Elias wasn't home, but then we heard him out back cussin' at something. Paw took the dog around back and asked for his money back. Well, first Cline claimed that Rattler wasn't the dog he sold Paw. Just then, one of the young'uns came out of the house and called the dog by name. When Cline was through cussin' the child, he next denied that there had been a trial period and said that he didn't want to buy the dog from Paw. Paw was awfully mad by then and said the he'd take his money out of Elias' hide if he couldn't get cash. Cline then threatened to take Paw to court if he tried. At that, Paw gave Rattler to the child who had claimed him, and we left. Paw refused to talk to anyone for the rest of the day. (He later said that he was so mad, he was afraid of what he might say or do.)

We found out later that Rattler would tree coons if he was hunting with a pack of hounds, but wouldn't leave the lights if there were only one or two dogs along. (I always reckoned he was afraid of the dark.) We also found out later that Cline sold Rattler "on trial" several times after he cheated us and that Elias pulled the same trick on all but his last victim.

The last one, a boot-legger from over in Wyoming County, pulled out a hawg-leg pistol and shot the dog AND Cline. "Miz Cline", as it turns out, was only a common-law wife and was not much better than Elias. She later left the children and ran off to Charleston with a pack-peddler.

You may ask if the problem with Cline could have been avoided by having a contract drawn up between the parties. The answer is "Probably not". I have always found that a man who won't honor a handshake won't pay any attention to a contract either, or at least no more attention than it takes to break it. Son, locks and contracts are for honest people. Thieves and scoundrels can break them when they want to do so.

Well, that's about all for this letter. Vicie has already rung the dinner bell twice, and the hounds'll get my part if I don't get down to the kitchen. Remember that we love you and are praying for you.

Love from your Dad,
William Anderson Hatfield

BUSINESS PRINCIPLE : It is possible to do a bad deal with good people, because that just happens sometimes. It is, however, impossible to do a good deal with bad people. If someone is honest only when you watch them closely, just think what they're probably doing where you do not see. Even if you aren't being cheated today, you are enabling that party to cheat someone else down the line.

I had an executive tell me once that "you can deal with the Devil if the contract is strong enough". He was ours, leading the effort to get a contractor to produce coal from a property owned by our employer. One of the bidders had been our coal supplier before, with a history of problems. This bidder, however, was offering a low price and did have an excellent relationship with top management, regardless of problems. The result was that we did not disqualify the bid (for poor performance in the past), so we spent the next seven years fighting every day to keep that supplier's hand out of our corporate pockets. At the end of that agreement, all of us celebrated, including that executive who then said that he had learned that no deal with the Devil is a good one because the Devil always cheats.

Oddly enough, the contractor noted above was unhappy during our relationship as well. If that team had put as much effort into mining coal for someone else as it did trying to get us to expand its rights under the contract, it would have finished that seven-year period in far better shape.

HISTORICAL NOTE : It was not at all uncommon in the mountains to buy a dog "on trial", whether it was a coon dog, a bird dog or otherwise. Because of the arduous labor put into subsistence farming, no farmer wanted to share the harvest with raccoons, groundhogs or other varmints (an Elizabethan corruption of vermin). Many in southern West Virginia kept dogs that would tree raccoons and then finish them off when they were shot out of the tree. Hides from animals thus taken were dried on the side of the barn and sold for much-needed "cash money". Having a good 'coon dog, therefore, was a necessity. The definition of "good" was one that did not chase rabbits, deer, foxes or other nocturnal creatures but would tree coons. Deer chasing dogs were of little use, since deer would often leave a trail that led to other watersheds, causing the farmer to waste time trying to find the dog. Such dogs not worth their feed, even scraps.

Pack peddlers sold dry goods from mountain door to door before the advent of passable roads. They would spend the night wherever they found shelter - home, barn, or otherwise. My grandmother used to tell us that more than one pack peddler was never seen again after spending the night at some cabins down in the hollows.

CHAPTER 5

PICK YOUR FIGHTS CAREFULLY; GRAVES ARE HARD TO DIG

Dear Sons:

I was restless all night and got up this morning to see the sun-rise. I guess the ones I have left to see would be easy to count by now. I took a jar of water from the springhouse, my satchel (that your Mother made me) with writing materials and walked up the hollow to that little waterfall I love so much. Sitting on the big rock there, I just took it all in – the trickle of the water, the stirring of the first birds, the rustle of some ground squirrels and, best of all, the change in the light. Looking down the hollow, I could see the horizon go from black to gray, then to gold. It made me think of the hearts of folks I've dealt with over the decades. Some good, some average and some as evil as can be. You have seen the same, and will be seeing more as the years go by.

There is a time to stand your ground and fight, a time to trade for what you want and a time to walk away, even if you believe you are in the right. Your grandfather and his father tried to teach me this when I was growing up, but I never appreciated what they had to say. Leastways, I didn't until my hands were red with the blood of folks on both sides of the Feud. I may have been able to stop it before it got out of hand, but I'll never know because I didn't try. I was too busy showing everyone that Anse Hatfield couldn't be pushed around. You lived through that nightmare and know what you need to do to keep it from happening again. Let Old Man Herbert Harmon be an example to you, the way he has for me in recent years.

Herbert Harmon (everybody called Old Man Herbert, so as not to confuse him with his boy, Young Herbert) lived over on Ben's Creek on what had to be one of the rockiest pieces of ground in Creation. He was also one of the most even-tempered men you would ever want to meet.

In fact, he had a real talent for settling disagreements just by talking things over with all the parties involved, so much so that people would bring him their disputes before they would take them to court. Old Man Herbert had a way of making you satisfied that the right thing was being done, even if the overall settlement went against you. A lot of folk wanted him to run for judge, but he refused on the grounds that politics was no place for an honest man and that he had no formal education. Maybe he was the better for it.

I recall one of the best examples of Mr. Harmon's peace-making was when Bill Bragg and Red Lee Browning, both from Gilbert Creek, had a falling out over a property line between their two farms. They agreed on the property corner down by the road, but some of Bragg's hogs had rooted up the back corner. Browning hired a surveyor to put it back, but both men came out with shotguns to see that the job was done right. The surveyor was ready to quit when Old Man Herbert, on his way home from Gilbert, happened by. Both land-owners asked him to see what he thought was right. What happened next was pure Harmon.

When he got off the mule, Old Man Herbert asked the surveyor if he could look through the transit, which was set up on the front corner and pointing up the hill. He then asked the surveyor's helper to go to the top of the hill and to be ready to put in a permanent marker. With everyone in place, Harmon motioned for the helper to move, first left and then right, several times before calling "Put it right there!". The surveyor was paid, and everyone was satisfied. After both farmers went back into the house, the surveyor asked Old Man Herbert where he had gotten surveying training. Harmon then told him that he had none and said, "The Lord knows that where that marker was put may be right or may be wrong. As your helper moved left and right, I watched Bill and Red's faces. Go one way, and one man would smile while the other frowned. The opposite happened if you went back the other way. I just had your man move until they both had the same expression on their faces. That was close enough for neighbors."

It never occurred to me until after Mr. Harmon had died just what helped make him the kind of man he was. Of course, the way he was raised had a lot to do with it, but I believe that the hardness of his land is what made him seek more reasonable solutions to the problems of life. When he died, a bunch of us who respected him volunteered to dig his grave on the point of the hill where his people were buried. Young Herbert held that it was his responsibility, but we convinced him to let us pay our respects in that way. He did prevail upon us to use his tools, which included a sledge-hammer, a big star chisel, a case of powder and some blasting caps. It was a good thing we did.

The point where the Harmon family had been buried for generations did not appear unusual except for having no trees. When we started digging, we were surprised to find that, beneath about 6 inches of topsoil and clay, there was a solid outcropping of sandstone thicker than a grave is deep. It took a dozen of us over 18 hours to finish the grave, which we squared off by lantern-light after sending twice for more powder. As we packed up to go, it struck me that, if all graves were that hard to dig, a man might grow up putting a greater value on life and being a lot more particular about how he chooses to settle his differences with others. When you boil it all down, life is too precious to waste it on senseless fighting.

Since Vicie will have someone looking for me soon, I'll close for now. Give those young'uns a hug from their Grampaw.

Love from your Dad,
William Anderson Hatfield.

BUSINESS PRINCIPLE : In a competitive world, conflict is to be expected. The successful leader will resist the temptation, internal and external, to fight with adversaries without carefully examining the issues, what is to be gained/lost by the struggle and whether or not it is possible to get what one wants, or most of it anyway, through negotiation. It is easy to win a battle while losing the war. It is harder to find ways to reach your goals through understanding your adversary's. Harder, but achievable.

I speak from sad experience when I say that it's not enough to be right in a conflict. If you go about demonstrating just how right you are in the wrong way, you will be ineffective and no one will care about how brilliant you were. Early in my career, my company had a number of operating subsidiaries who bought coal. My boss and I worked for a subsidiary which provided multiple services to the operating companies, including monitoring coal contracts entered into by those operating sub's. Several of those were "cost-plus" contracts, where my company had joined a number of other companies to provide capital to develop coal mines and to pay all of the expenses for those mines. Two coal companies held those "cost-plus" contracts. One was conscientious and kept costs as low as it could. The other one was geared towards maximizing profits, regardless of cost. The second one was also adept at belonging to the same clubs and churches as our buyers and making those buyers feel important. The result was that my company's customers paid way too much for the product we provided and my boss and I made ourselves unwelcome at the operating sub's because we couldn't understand how those folks were loyal to their vendor. Ultimately, changes were made, but they came after we were gone.

HISTORICAL NOTE : Many families in southern West Virginia had their cemeteries on the hillside behind or above their homes. As noted earlier, flat land was to be farmed. Where a ridge slopes down between two hollows, that is called a point. Vince Gill's "Go Rest High On That Mountain" is a beautiful depiction of such a family cemetery. Often, friends and neighbors would dig graves when someone passed, sparing the family the necessity of digging it themselves. When digging by hand, they did whatever was needed to put things in order.

CHAPTER 6

GIVEN THE RIGHT STIMULUS, PEOPLE CAN CHANGE

Dear Sons :

We had a good church service this morning, although Brother Deke Davis might have done better if he'd left out a couple of the minor prophets and at least one of the Apostle Paul's missionary journeys. He was preaching on changed lives, and he knows more about that than most men. That brings to me the next thing I wanted to pass along to you.

Deke Davis (short for Deacon) was not always the kind of man you'd want to see behind a pulpit. His parents had named him in hopes of his being as active in the church as they were. He busted loose early, however, and went as far over the line the other way as he could. In grammar school, he got one too many switchings and burned down the schoolhouse. He then intimidated the teacher out of pressing charges, a little man who quit and took to pig farming shortly thereafter. Deke worked odd jobs to get drinking money while expecting his mother and invalid father to support him. Yet, in all of that, they never quit praying for him, especially when he took the job of driving wagon-loads of corn whiskey over into Virginia for Hobart Mounts.

Hobart Mounts was then one of the biggest bootleggers in this part of the country. He was a hard man, with ten to fifteen little coal mines, each with its own moonshine still. His young'uns took out enough coal to fire the stills and to sell a little coal on the side. This left room underground for the moonshine operations in places most people wouldn't think to look for them. All that was missing was a man to haul corn and sugar up to the mines and demi-johns of white lightning away (in a wagon with a false bottom). That was where Deke came in.

Mounts started Deke out slowly, probably because he wasn't sure how far he could trust a nineteen-year-old boy who was already a hard drinker. The first wagon runs were to carry supplies to the mines and "product" to the central collection point – a big sawmill out along the ridge from Twisted Gun Gap. After several months without incident, Hobart put Deke on his Hurley, Virginia run with a big wagon built to look like it was loaded with lumber (but with 150 gallons of "white lightning" inside). Because the distance was only about 35 miles, the wagon would leave the mill at about 8 AM, be in Hurley by about 1 PM, get unloaded while Deke got a bite to eat and then be back to the mill by about 6 PM (a little faster when unloaded). It wasn't too demanding a job, except for the occasional search by a deputy sheriff whose monthly payment from Mounts was late. (They never found any whiskey, but did frequently take whatever pocket money Deke had on him.) The only other challenge Deke faced was the concern about traveling through Twisted Gun Gap long past sundown.

The wagon road over Twisted Gun Gap is no small task even in daylight, because of the steep grade and several hairpin turns. The middle third of it was the worst. It was a narrow section, blasted out of the cliff, with a rock wall on one side and a sheer drop on the other. It lay just beyond a spring that the Indians said was haunted. The legend held that two Shawnee braves were camped by that spring one night back during the French & Indian War, when something big and black circled their camp, just beyond the fire-light. After it had circled several times, it moved off down the mountain. The braves then took torches and what little they had, including an old flint-lock rifle, and lit out for the mountain-top. By the light of the full moon, they found their way to the low point on the ridge, the gap, where the black thing waited.

Days later, one of the Indians was found wandering along about 10 miles away, drooling and staring into space. Every hair on his head was snow-white. His kinsmen back-tracked him to the gap and found a pile of ashes with some bits of bone and human teeth. They also found the rifle, with the barrel twisted along its length like you would wring out a rag. Since then, the location has been known as Twisted Gun Gap. At least, that's how Deke heard the story.

It had been a very long day when Deke started the team of mules up the mountain. The wagon had lost a steel tire halfway to Hurley. By the time Davis had put the tire back on, driven into a stream and then waited for the wooden wheel to swell to fit, he was 4 hours late. Mounts' buyer, fearing the worst, had closed his store at 5 and had to be fetched back to unload the wagon. What with one thing and the other, it was 11 PM when Deke started up the hill.

While waiting in Hurley, he bought a nice dinner and a jug of whiskey (bought whiskey, since one did NOT steal from Mounts). About half of the jug was left when Deke saw the full moon peeping over the mountain-top. In the pale glow, shadows of large trees crept across the road ahead, and the dark hollow seemed to move a bit, like something blowing in the wind. Nervously, he whipped the mules up a little faster. Deke breathed a little better until he hit the hairpin curve leading into the road cut, just past the old spring.

At the curve, the mules slowed, and Deke heard something big leave the brush and start up the road behind the wagon. He tried to empty his old Army revolver at the sound, but not one chamber would fire. He then screamed at the mules and began to whip them furiously. As they entered the cut, they began to run, with no place to go but straight ahead. Just then, the rear end of the wagon sank down as if a heavy load had been dropped on it. The mules struggled wildly with driving legs, but the wagon slowed to a crawl.

Deke dropped to his belly at the front of the wagon and crawled under the seat. He then felt the weight on the back of the wagon shift as something moved forward. On it came, until the springs on the wagon seat were compressed completely. The mules were snorting strings of foam with each breath. Then, Deke saw something big and black blot out the moon as it flowed off the front of the wagon, down between the maddened mules and then off the edge of the cliff. As the weight left the wagon, the mules took off like being shot from a cannon. Deke had to make himself climb back onto the wagon seat and to steer the team off onto the sawmill access road at the top of the hill, where he fell into the arms of a surprised Hobart Mounts and resigned. At the boy's tearful insistence, the two built a roaring fire and fed it with slab wood until dawn.

The next morning was Sunday, and Deke amazed his folks by entering the church door, walking the aisle and asking to be baptized immediately. It was an answer to prayer for which they were forever grateful, even if it was a little scary to see their son walk into that church with the finest head of snow-white hair you ever saw. Deke later became a deacon and then pastor of our little church. While he has never talked much about his conversion, he keeps that old pistol, the one with the twisted barrel, over his fireplace and occasionally takes it down and polishes it when trial and temptations come his way.

Sons, you and I are also examples of how a man may turn from old practices and habits and begin a new life. Consider that when you are dealing with folks there in the courthouse. Given the right stimulus, a person, deputy or criminal, can change. Don't write anyone off too quickly.

Love from your Dad,
William Anderson Hatfield

BUSINESS PRINCIPLE : Properly motivated, anyone can change. Some will change based on the hope of better things ahead. Others need a glimpse of something bad coming towards them. Whichever is the case, when you align that person's self-interest with your own, good things can happen. See that you give them all a fair chance before taking punitive action.

CHAPTER 7

SOMETIMES, YOU CAN'T PLEASE ANYONE BUT YOURSELF

Dear Sons:

The weather is cold and damp this morning, which means that the aches and pains from old bullet wounds, broken bones and stiff joints have put me in a chair beside the fire. I do declare that getting old is not for cowards. Vicie can't feel too much better than me, but she is just bustling around here keeping the house going. That little girl from up the holler, Icy Pearl, is helping her today. A sad story, that one, but smart and willing to work. She'll meet the right boy and make a good wife someday.

Looking at the fire puts me to mind of the time that Leander Blankenship nearly got shot by his mother-in-law. This being a border area, there were some of us on both sides in the War, and some families didn't take kindly to having their daughters courted by a young man whose family wore the wrong color. This was especially true of the Smith family from Buffalo Creek, who had kinfolk in Charlottesville and a pretty daughter named Emmaline. She was courted by Leander Blankenship, whose uncle had been with Sheridan in the Virginia campaign. Needless to say, there was no love lost between her people and his. She was an only child, though, and prevailed upon her father to give his blessing for their marriage. After that, things got downright interesting.

While Leander worked on building the cabin that he and Emmaline would call home, she worked on getting her mother to give at least grudging acceptance to Leander's existence. By the time everything but the chimney was built, Mother Smith no longer wanted to horse-whip the young man, but was still pretty cool towards him. She even softened to the point where she gave Emmaline an heirloom set of dining room chairs for the new cabin. Now, this cabin didn't have a dining room, but that didn't bother the young prospective bride. However, it was on the day that Leander hauled them up to the cabin that disaster struck.

The new Blankenship cabin sat out on a ridge between Jake's Branch and Horsepen Creek. While secluded, it had a fine spring, a beautiful view and wasn't all that far from the wagon roads to Logan, Gilbert or even Williamson. It also lay within the territory of a pair of panthers, a fact that sort of surprised Leander when he found out about it. His brothers had taken him and those eight chairs up to the cabin early in the morning and had then taken their wagon on to Gilbert to get a keg of nails for the barn and also a chimney damper that was being built by the blacksmith there. Leander was left behind with a few tools to finish the chimney, but forgot to get his rifle out from under the wagon seat.

The firebox and hearth for the fireplace had been laid and the chimney completed just about as high as a man could reach flat-footed. A pile of dressed stones and a ladder lay outside. Leander had just carried all the chairs inside, and had begun to mix a fresh batch of mortar when he heard what sounded like a woman screaming - the cry of a panther. His hair stood on end.

Grabbing a hatchet as his only protection, Leander ran inside the cabin and got the door barred just as something hit it. He then quickly latched the shuttered windows and the back door as well. During all of this, the panther kept screaming as it circled the cabin returning from time to time to scratch at the front door. Leander hoped that it would go away until he heard scratching around the chimney. In a panic, he ran to the hearth, struck a spark into some wood shavings and got a fire started. Leander then realized that the only wood he had in the cabin was a handful of kindling, a couple of shelf boards and his future mother-in-law's eight precious chairs.

Leander considered his choices. He couldn't block the chimney with chairs because it was too big. He couldn't fight the panther with only a hatchet unless it was his last hope. But, then again, the prospect of facing Mother Smith with nothing but the ashes of her great grand-mother's chairs made a good old panther and hatchet fight look better by the minute. It was when he heard the second panther scream at the door and then join its mate moaning at the chimney that he decided he must be worth more to Emmaline than furniture.

After some hair-raising trial and error with the shelf boards, Leander learned just how small his fire could be and still keep the lions away from the throat of the chimney. He used all of the kindling, the boards and a few feebly burning strips of wood chopped from the cabin call first, hoping that the cats would lose interest. Unfortunately, the panthers were now invested in the effort and seemed determined to get a hearty meal of Blankenship.

It turns out that heirloom chairs which have been hand-polished for about a hundred years with bee's-wax and Lord-knows-what-else make dandy fuel, especially the legs with the lion-claw ends and the backs carved in a collection of scenes from the Old Testament. Leander fed them into the fire, one scrap at a time, for hours and prayed harder with each stick. He was getting ready to break up the last two chairs when he heard a rifle-shot and then shouting. A few minutes later, his brother beat on the front door and called for the young man to come out. Leander took a look at the ashes of the six chairs, sighed and then opened the door.

The first thing striking about the front porch was the series of deep gashes in the front door and door frame (there to this day). The second thing was the carcass of a large male mountain lion stretched at the feet of a smiling, rifle-toting Boyd Blankenship. Their brother, Newsome, was standing by the harnessed mules, which were still trembling with fear.

The Blankenship boys hunted that second lion for weeks before deciding that it must have left the country. Mother Smith took to her bed when she found out about the chairs and wasn't able to leave it until well after the wedding. She couldn't look at Leander without clenching her fists, until the night Emmaline gave birth to their first son, whom the proud father promptly named William (after Mother Smith's father). After that, she softened up some. The two surviving chairs, with pictures of Daniel in the Lion's Den and Noah building the Ark, were put into a place of honor by the front window of the cabin, with a handsome panther-skin rug between them. Sometimes on a dark night, Leander would tell his children how a man has to act when he's between a rock and a hard place.

Love from your Dad,
William Anderson Hatfield

BUSINESS PRINCIPLE : There will be times when you find yourself in a tight spot, where somebody is going to think you are wrong, no matter what you may do. It is then that you have to examine each option critically and then choose the one you believe to be the right thing to do. It may not always be the most profitable or the easiest, but it will be the right path. If you are going to get shot at anyway, might as well suit yourself. I strongly believe that being fired for doing the right thing is better than being promoted when you do wrong. My grandmother, when I was misbehaving and trying to hide it, always used to quote a portion of Numbers 32:23 "be sure your sin will find you out". Do the right thing, and be able to sleep well at night.

HISTORICAL NOTE : Leander Blankenship was my great-grandfather. I have taken a few liberties with the story, but it was told to me by my father's mother, Icy Pearl Blankenship in the basic outline used above.

CHAPTER 8

A MAN CONVINCED AGAINST HIS WILL. . . ISN'T

Dear Sons:

I noticed in your last letter that you are all starting to get annoyed with the politicians there in the courthouse, as well as your county's delegates to Charleston. While your frustration is totally understandable, your expectations are too high. Many of those officials are looking out for themselves or some sponsor and also being bombarded with ideas and requests from all sides. They tend not to like conflict, and will agree with you to your face then agree with the next guy they meet as well, even if you and that fellow have opposite views. Truth be told (as it rarely is in such matters), the politician probably doesn't agree with either of you. When you really convince a person, he or she will hold onto that position. If they act convinced just to get away from you (or to get something away from you), they will revert to the position they had before you came along. A man convinced against his will. . . . is of the same opinion still.

It reminds me of Jess Miller, from over at Chattaroy. Jess was a bachelor in his 40's, who lived in a small cabin not far up Chattaroy holler. He was a friendly, happy man; although a mite homely and coarse, so not many women showed any interest in him until Sadie Tiller came to the Tug Valley to stay with her aunt. Sadie was in her 40's as well, and was also sort of homely. (Your mother says she had a sweet personality, but that just verifies my description.) She had been hunting for a husband for some years at that point, without success. I guess you could say that Jess was a consolation prize.

They met at church, where Sadie noticed his stained shirt and a tear in his pants leg that needed repair. She also noticed his dirty fingernails, but her top discovery was that he wore no rings, on any finger of either hand. The next Sunday, she brought him a pie. After that, it was a basket lunch that she asked him to share at the all-day-singing-and-dinner-on-the-ground service. Jess had never eaten so well in his life, and he was bright enough not to let a good thing get away.

They were married in the fall, and Sadie immediately took Jess on as a project. She cleaned all the garbage and assorted bachelor junk (by her definition only) out of his cabin, sewed him some new shirts, made him buy some new, more stylish clothes and then made him start bathing regularly. Son, that fellow was sparkly clean when they came to church, and all of the ladies in the congregation remarked at how nice their cabin looked, both inside and out. You'd think Jess would have been elated, but (aside from putting on a few pounds) he never smiled any more, just looked miserable.

It turns out that Sadie's training method for Jess (as told to one of her friends in the Women's Fellowship group) was to have him sleep in the loft of the cabin any time his behavior did not meet with her approval. The cabin was small, so the loft was the only other place he could sleep and stay warm on those cold winter nights. Little by little, he changed his ways until she could see her way clear to let him back into the bed. He agreed to do things her way, but it would be a mistake to say that he was convinced.

Things went more or less smoothly (given the things unsaid between them) until the month of February rolled around. Sadie got word that her aunt had taken sick and needed her to come over to McCarr, Kentucky to take care of her. In the two months that passed, Jess began to lose his shine. He started wearing overalls and flannel shirts again, and began to look a little more wrinkled. His beard re-appeared, and his overall appearance began to look more like the Jess Miller we all knew. Not only that, but he started to look happier, at least until she wrote to tell him to pick her up in Matewan on the first of April.

Based on what Sadie's aunt's neighbors told us later, Jess showed up in Matewan with his wagon and mule. In the back of the wagon was Sadie's sewing machine and the rest of her belongings that had been left in the cabin. Jess knocked on the front door and announced that Sadie had to make a choice. Did she want to be married to him and work out some basic principles for their living together or did she want to live with everything done her way? In the first case, he was prepared to put what she had brought with her into the wagon and take her home. In the second, he was prepared to unload the wagon right there and go home alone. She was shocked because she had been sure that she had convinced him that her ways were best. Needless to say, he wasn't sold on that idea.

In the weeks and months that followed, most of the folks at that church allowed as to how both Sadie and Jess looked happier after that. Jess kept his beard, although it was nicely trimmed. His clothes got less wrinkled, but continued to be predominantly flannel shirts and overalls, with the occasional linen shirt worn with his broadcloth suit. Those visiting the cabin remarked that it once again looked like a man lived there with Sadie. The tablecloth and doilies were still there, but so were the deer antlers and guns hung over the fireplace. Jess closed off the inside loft entrance and moved the ladder outside, where it gave access to a new door cut into the gable end of the cabin. It gave new meaning to "these two shall become one", as read during the marriage ceremony. They had spent those first months trying to figure out "which one" and then learned that the "one" the preacher was talking about was to be the best of both parties. Of that, they were both firmly convinced.

Well, it's getting late and time to bank the fire for the night. I hope you can benefit from this story as you deal with those elected officials. You can't force your ideas on them. They have to "want" to try them, and some version of the idea that gets both of you what you want will probably be the one they will stick to.

Love from your Dad,
William Anderson Hatfield

BUSINESS PRINCIPLE : You can achieve more through consensus than through imposing your will on others. They may say what you want to hear in person, but you can never be sure that the person maneuvered into agreeing with you really does. Compromise may seem like a dirty word to some, but you can get what you want when you can find a way to help others do the same thing. A person convinced against his or her will. . . .isn't.

HISTORICAL NOTE : Back then, as now, there were a number of people who lived alone through no fault of their own. Bachelors kept cabins in the woods and pretty much suited themselves unless they happened to meet someone who caught their eye. Spinsters (an archaic term for an unmarried woman, usually too old to have her age counted on fingers and toes) lived with family, or occasionally alone, and (in many cases) looked for a man they could love and respect. Church services were an important part of life, and provided an opportunity to meet unattached persons of the opposite sex. Human nature being what it is, folks at those churches who were already married took advantage of every opportunity to "fix up" a friend with someone with "a sweet personality" whom they thought was a perfect match for that friend. I had a buddy once who declared that he wanted everyone to be married, because it wasn't fair for anyone to be happier than he was. His wife was a sweet, beautiful and very patient woman.

Politicians have not changed in the last 100 years, the technology has just gotten better. I propose that we remove all limits on campaign contribution, but make politicians wear NASCAR-type coveralls identifying just for whom they are working. Truth in advertising.

CHAPTER 9

YOU ARE ONLY LEADING IF SOMEONE IS FOLLOWING

Dear Sons :

It was interesting seeing that picture in the newspaper of Joe and the Mayor of Logan greeting that Army officer last week. It was hard to tell from the quality of that black-and-white picture, but his uniform sure did look purty. He had enough ribbons, braids and such to make your mother a hat. I hope the visit went well, especially given the nature of representatives from the federal government who offer to "help" us. Those folks always seem to do well even if they are up to no good. He resembled someone I knew during the War, but didn't look quite old enough to be that man, nor would I expect the man I remember to show up in a Yankee uniform, not after what happened to him.

Captain Beauregard Philemon Cottonseed was in charge of the unit in which I served during the War Between the States. I believe his daddy bought him a captain's commission, expecting that young Beau would distinguish himself on the battlefield and return a general. He had a lovely gray uniform, with gold buttons and braid, an ostrich-feathered hat and a gray cape with a red satin lining. With yellow hair, mutton-chop whiskers and ice-blue eyes, he sure looked the part. He proved, however, not to be worth the powder it would take to blow him up.

Captain Beau, as the camp ladies called him, treated all of his subordinates, from lieutenant on down, equally poorly. He walked around with an "I-smell-dung" expression on his face and spoke to you with his eyes focused on a spot just over your right shoulder. He knew no one's name, claiming that men came and went so quickly it was just a waste of time to try to remember "who was whom". If a venture went well, he would chew us all out for what mistakes he believed we made (mistakes that prevented faster victory or greater glory) and then took credit for all that was accomplished by his unit. If something went badly, he made it clear that he was ashamed of us and then passed up the line all the reasons why the failures were not his own.

Captain "Cotton-picker", as we came to call him, had no concept of military strategy and would not accept suggestions from peer or subordinate. On the occasions where we were victorious, it was because some sergeant or lieutenant chose to "misunderstand" orders and then carry on successfully. If he had left nothing to the imagination, we obeyed foolish orders and paid for it with high losses. Indeed, there was high turn-over in the unit because of unnecessary deaths, maimed soldiers and, in extreme cases, desertion. The captain was the last man up the hill in a charge and the first one down the hill in retreat. He rode a beautiful white gelding for a while, until it was killed by a stray bullet (although it was rumored that the horse got shot accidentally by one of our guys who was holding just a little too low). After that, he rode whatever horse might be available and stayed a little farther behind the front lines.

One night, after a short, ugly retreat, we decided that we'd had enough. The counter-attack was being planned for the next morning and we knew that, once more, Captain Cotton-picker would arrange to have his unit at the toughest point on the line of attack. We believed that we had a fair chance of success because General John Morgan had issued each officer specific orders, written on muslin, with instructions to memorize and then burn them. We did not know that our captain, after passing them along verbally, saved his orders to use when he went to the latrine, nor did we know that one of the camp women was a Yankee spy who retrieved them. After a bit of washing, the Yankee commander holding the hill up which we would charge was able to prepare a surprise for our good captain, but it paled in comparison to the surprise we had for our glorious leader.

The morning began according to plan, with everyone awake and ready to move before dawn. What little gear we had was quietly stowed, and our campfires were left burning to mask the fact that we were on the move. Captain Cottonseed climbed onto his big grey mare, not knowing that the man who had saddled it for him had cut the cinch strap mostly through, leaving only enough threads to survive his mounting and some gently walking movements by the horse. He positioned himself where he thought our rear line would be and then issued the command to move forward, which we obeyed.

At first, we were as quiet as possible, waiting until we were upon an unsuspecting enemy to unleash the famed Rebel Yell. That first line of Yankee skirmishers seemed surprised and quickly retreated towards the hill-top. We followed in hot pursuit, only to be greeted by hot lead from several hundred defenders dug in behind stumps, logs and piles of rocks. Our success quickly turned into a rout, and we were driven back down the hill followed by screaming blue-bellies. Still, because of the fog, our overall losses were light, so we retreated in as orderly a manner as possible – retreated right past our peerless captain who, seeing us and the Yankees coming from the fog, yanked the mare's head around and spurred her to safety. At that moment, the cinch strap gave up the ghost, leaving the captain and his silver-mounted saddle sitting there on the ground. With the fall, his saber and cape got tangled with the saddle mountings and he was unable to effect an orderly retreat along with us. The last that any of us saw of him, he was surrounded by blue-coated soldiers with his hands in the air.

We heard later that Captain Beauregard Philemon Cottonseed spent the rest of the war in a camp near Erie, Pennsylvania. Some said that his name came up in discussion of a prisoner exchange for officers, but that the Confederate representative to the talks declined the trade.

Sons, you are only a leaders when people are willing to follow you. You can't command their loyalty or buy it. You must earn it, by sharing most of the credit when you have success and taking most of the blame when you do not. When your people see that you care about their interests and their lives as well as your own and that you aren't willing to ask them to do something you are unwilling to set yourself to, they will reward you by following your lead. If they aren't following you, you are not a leader, you are just taking a walk.

Speaking of a walk, your mother wants me to meander down the creek and see if I can find that duck of hers that keeps wandering away. If you ask me, we need a duck dinner on Sunday. Still, if Vicie isn't happy, I won't be either.

Love from your Dad,
William Anderson Hatfield.

BUSINESS PRINCIPLE : Never confuse management with leadership. Management is the impersonal implementation of plans and the coordination of materials and labor to accomplish an objective. It is important to business because it gets results, but has its limitations. When a good manager, who knows the nuts and bolts of getting things done, is also a leader whom people want to follow and whom people want to see succeed, he or she will ALWAYS accomplish more than a mere manager. You manage materials and robots. You must LEAD people if you want your unit to reach its potential. When people feel pushed instead of led, unpleasant things can happen, both to them and to those who supervise them. Watch that cinch strap!

HISTORICAL NOTE : Devil Anse Hatfield was a Confederate soldier, and more than a few of the officers on both sides of the Civil War had commissions bought by themselves or their families. Many aspired to political office later in life, and time spent on the battlefield would prove valuable in those ventures, so long as the officer could stay alive and untarnished.

CHAPTER 10

ALWAYS COUNT THE MONEY YOURSELF

Dear Sons :

I wish you all well with your investigation of embezzlement and corruption in the Town of Logan. Some people would be shocked to see what goes on behind the closed doors of those with power of any sort, be it political or otherwise. Many a good man has fallen prey to the idea that he has enough power to do whatever he pleases. That road leads to corruption, disgrace and, possibly, death. An old friend once told me that any man who will lie to you will also steal from you if he gets a chance. Given the number of lies that politicians get used to telling, they're just a short step away from stealing whatever they think they can get away with. So, go get the folks who've been dipping into the public purse. However, also be wary of the temptations yourself and ALWAYS make sure that you count the money that anyone else is holding or managing for you.

Some time ago, two fellows I knew decided to get into the business of selling coal. Their grandad had left them several parcels of adjoined land, along with the mineral rights to the coal there. It was in the Eagle coal seam, which is known for good quality and decent mining conditions. One of the cousins, Jepthah Taylor, was a hard worker with a knack for leading others and managing projects. The other cousin, Clayburne Lester, had a good head for figures and worked at the local bank. They made the perfect inside/outside team for running a business that is long on physical labor. Each put up $5,000 and agreed to share costs and profits equally.

You might think that mining a big block of Eagle coal that was eight feet thick would be like printing money. In this case, you would be wrong.

When the mine had a really good month and was able to sell every lump of coal it mined, they were able to pay the bills, make payroll and have a few hundred dollars left to split. When there was a short month financially, they wound up having to put those few hundred dollars back into the business to keep going. At the end of five years, Jepthah had made back only about one tenth of his original investment, and he was sort of depressed.

One big problem was that Jepthah stayed so busy running the coal mine that he never had time to study the books. The other big problem was that Clayburne was keeping two sets of books anyway. You see, the coal reserves they were mining outcropped (came to the surface) on both sides of a big ridge, in different watersheds. Unbeknownst to Jepthah, Clayburne hired a third party to start a second mine on the other side of the mountain. When he bought a case of blasting powder for Mine No. 1, he also bought one for Mine No. 2 and charged it to the one they shared. At the end of five years, Clayburne had made enough money from Mine No. 2 to pack up and move to a fine old home in Richmond, Virginia. From there, he continued to run the business side of the joint venture and might have done so for several more years if it hadn't been for a mistake by the contractor in Mine No. 2. It seems that, instead of turning left and mining away from Mine No. 1, the contractor turned right and cut right into the other mine. After that, it didn't take a genius to figure out what was happening.

The upshot of it all is that the contractor in Mine No. 2 didn't have any evidence directly implicating Clayburne and, so, went to jail alone. Not long after that, however, Clayburne's house in Richmond was broken into one night, and Clayburne was killed. With no heirs and no will, his fortune reverted to Jepthah, his only living relative, who just happened to be in town. Mine No. 1 continued operating (alone in the reserve this time) for another 10 years, during which time Jepthah ALWAYS took time to inspect the books being kept by a hired accountant. In later years, Jepthah was a fixture in Richmond society, and nearly everyone who was anyone was frequently a guest in that fine old mansion.

Boys, Jesus handpicked Judas Iscariot to be His disciple and to keep the common purse that was used to meet the needs of the Master as He went about in ministry. I am sure, however, that He knew exactly how much money was in that purse at any time and how often Judas may have dipped into the bag. Always, I say always, keep track of the money yourself, no matter how many others are helping you count it. If there is something foul going on in that courthouse, a careful tracking of the money (in and out) will help you find the truth.

Doc Chafin just got here to see your mother. She's been a little consumptive for the last few days, and I'm worried about her. Little Icy Pearl has been helping out as much as she can, but the house just doesn't run right without Vicie's hand in all that goes on. Take care of yourself, and I'll let you know how your mother is next letter.

Love from your Dad,
William Anderson Hatfield.

BUSINESS PRINCIPLE : An honest accountant is a crucial part of every successful business venture. The story has been told of a company looking for a new Chief Financial Officer. As they interviewed candidates, their final question was always "How much is 2 + 2?" Most of those job seekers quickly answered "Four" and were passed over. When the final candidate was asked the same question, his response was to lock the door, draw the drapes, sweep the room for bugs and then answer "How much do you want it to be?", whereupon he was hired. It's a cute story, but is not good business. Eventually, the truth about a business' numbers will be revealed publically. If that revelation shows illegal accounting activities (or ones which, while technically legal, served to mislead others into putting hard-earned funds into a failure), it is highly likely that those involved in those shifty activities are going to suffer. Some will simply lose their jobs, pensions, perks, etc. Others will go to jail.

Quite a few questionable schemes in recent years are like a guy who starts the day with ten pockets, each holding a ten dollar bill. Through the course of the day, he transfers money from pocket to pocket as quickly and as often as he can. At the end of the day, he expects you to believe that he now has $110 on him. It is amazing that he can get others to let him move their money around too. Beware the deal that sounds too good to be true, promising more in return than most other people get. There are most likely risks involved that someone is not telling you about. Always look at the financials with a jaundiced eye, checking everything twice, then again. A good deal will survive scrutiny.

HISTORICAL NOTE : There are more anecdotes about rotten business dealings than you can shake a stick at. The coal business is particularly full of them. Several large coal companies over the years found themselves owning mines and equipment that had been bought with their own funds and operated without their knowledge. The old trick of buying "one for you and one for me" with your money was a common practice in the twentieth century. I can think of three companies/subsidiaries born from such thievery. In every case, someone lost his/her job and most or all of the fortune that had been gained through deceit.

The Eagle seam is an excellent seam of coal that lies in southern West Virginia and has been highly sought-after over the years. It is not unusual for a coal seam to outcrop in adjacent water-sheds and have mines on both sides of the mountain. Island Creek Coal Company mined a seam called Guyan Eagle for many years and actually had three mines which cut in together under the mountain-top. I worked in one of them when first starting in the field. Special care has to be taken with ventilation in those cases, but it can be done, usually intentionally.

CHAPTER 11

NEVER FIGHT WITH A VARMINT

Dear Sons:

Your mother is fine, just a little under the weather. The little girl from down the hollow has been a big help to her and is a blessing. So far, we haven't missed a meal, have clean clothes when we need them and the house is relatively clean. Still, I'll be happy when she is fully recovered.

We've seen in the paper how the people you're investigating in the courthouse are trying to accuse the three of you of what they've been doing. It's tempting to want to answer them in anger, but the best course of action is to be totally open with the public and to let the numbers speak for you. Trying to go nose to nose in a fight with a varmint is never a good plan. Just ask Rufus Hensley.

Rufus was a good old man who lived up Little Muncy Hollow off of Pigeon Creek. He raised chickens and the corn that he fed them. They provided eggs, meat and the occasional batch of baby chicks for which the store in Delbarton paid him. He wasn't rich, but he and his family had all they needed. All went well until he noticed that egg production was dropping off and that some of the hens were missing. A careful inspection of the hen-house showed a gap in the foundation through which a small animal could pass. Tracks in a muddy spot inside the coop were too small to be a raccoon, and Rufus suspected that he might have a weasel on his hands.

On the next trip to Delbarton, Rufus bought a small sack of cement, which he combined with some sand to make mortar. Using stones from the creek, he sealed the thief's access point. All was well for a couple of days, when he discovered that the varmint had dug underneath the wall of the hen-house and stolen another chicken. This was costing him serious money.

The next Saturday, Rufus bought two traps that would be suitable for a weasel and set them outside the hen-house, baited with some scraps. The next morning found the traps sprung, the baits gone and no trapped animal. What added insult to injury was the fact that he was also missing yet another one of his white chickens. This made him determined to beat the animal, so he put a trap inside and outside of the hole under the wall that night. When the sun came up, he found both traps sprung by sticks and the remains of half a dozen eggs on the floor beneath the nesting boxes. Now it was war, and Rufus was determined to win it.

This being no ordinary varmint, Rufus got some advice from his 90-year-old grandfather about how to set traps in ways that animals are not likely to detect. He put the traps in a bucket of chicken manure, along with a pair of old gloves. Both traps were set just inside the access hole, with everything but the trigger plates covered with litter from the hen-house floor. He wore the manure-soaked gloves as he set the traps. He then moved all of the chickens but one to a coop he had thrown together in the barn. These preparations done, Rufus armed himself with his hawg-leg pistol and a carbide light, and then spent the night sitting on an empty nail keg in the corner of the hen-house furthest from the traps. His only companion that night was an old hen who was marked for the next "chicken & dumplings" dinner that Rufus' wife would be cooking. All was in readiness.

Once the sun went down, the farm got fairly quiet. First to sleep was the old hen. Gradually, the cows quit lowing in the shed and the mule brayed his farewell to the sun. The dogs growled a couple of times, but then got quiet. After about six hours, Rufus heard something scratch against the foundation of the building, then some sniffing about. This was followed by a couple more scratching sounds and, finally, the snap of one of the traps. With a quick motion, Rufus lit the carbide light, leaped to his feet, drew down on the location of the trap with his pistol and yelled, "Gotcha, you sorry varmint!" The next few seconds went by like months, as the trapped mother skunk and her three offspring gasped, growled and turned about face. Before Rufus could get off a shot or even think to pull the trigger, he found himself sprayed, top to bottom, with a hideous fluid that seemed magnified by the relatively close quarters in the hen-house. Gagging furiously, Rufus crashed through the door to the building and ran for the creek, hoping to wash some of the spray out of his eyes. In the process, he dropped the carbide light into the straw on the floor of the coop, and the accumulated litter caught fire.

By the time he got his eyes clear, the retching Rufus saw his hen-house fully engulfed in flame and, in the light of the fire, saw the old hen staggering across the barnyard towards him AND also four skunks high-tailing it for the woods. After the ashes had cooled, he found only one trap, leading him to believe that the mother skunk had dragged the other away with her.

That was it for Rufus! He sold all of his chickens but the one to a man a couple of hollows over and took to raising pigs. His wife burned the clothes, belt and boots he was wearing that night. Rufus shaved his head and beard as well and used three bars of lye soap in a tub of water barely cooled enough to avoid burns. He also replaced the wood grips on the pistol with ones he carved himself. He was mostly none the worse for wear, except you couldn't stand close to him in wet weather for the next five years. His wife said she just got used to it, but her sense of smell was never the same. The old hen was allowed the run of the place until she died of odorous old age.

Fellows, I know you will be careful and will watch your temper. It's just so hard to do when someone you know to be a fool or a thief (or both) is mouthing off about something wrong you didn't do. When those days come, just remember Rufus. You may not have known his name, but he was that tall fellow with the surprised look you met on Election Day.

Love from your Dad,
William Anderson Hatfield.

BUSINESS PRINCIPLE : A common tactic used by someone caught on the wrong side of an argument is to attack his/her opponent. Many times, that person will accuse you of whatever wrong-doing or mistake that he or she was engaging in at the time. If this person can get you to respond in anger, then your argument is lost. Impartial observers will conclude either that both of you are guilty of malfeasance or that you do not have proof of your position that will withstand scrutiny. It then devolves into a "He Said/She Said" discussion where nothing will be accomplished, perhaps permanently. There is a time for a firm response in one's own defense. Far better to have such an abundance of evidence at hand that one can respond strictly with the facts, stripped of emotion. The opponent is then most likely either to grow more strident in attacking you or to capitulate. In either case, an impartial observer will conclude that your position is reasoned and sound.

HISTORICAL NOTE : Eggs, butter and smoked meat were the currency used by many mountain families to get the staples they couldn't grow or kill, such as salt, flour, etc. My maternal grandmother sold eggs to get extra money she could use for household needs or to provide small prizes for her Sunday School class. I won a fifty-cent piece at the age of 5 for memorizing the 23rd Psalm. My paternal grandmother sold butter to a local store-keeper, causing my father to hate butter-milk, for that was the only kind of milk they kept. My paternal grandfather hunted squirrels year-round with a .22 rifle and sold them to richer folks (which at that time was nearly everybody else around) who wanted some variety in their protein intake.

My hunting buddy, Herb, once got skunk scent on his head (accidentally) and, climbing into bed late that night, shocked his wife out of a deep sleep, since shampooing just enhanced the fragrance.

CHAPTER 12

DON'T MAKE A DECISION WHEN YOU ARE ANGRY

Dear Sons :

Doc Chafin just left, having told me he'd be surprised if I make it until his next visit. While Levicy and I got our affairs in order some time ago, I'm going to miss these letters I've been writing you. Some might consider them the ramblings of an old man, but these stories carry a message nonetheless. Since this may be my last letter, I don't want it to end without passing along what may be the most important lesson I've learned in life. Never make a decision when you are angry, because you may set in motion things you cannot stop. Nothing in my life exemplifies that more than the feud. I hate that word. So easily said, but so deceptive in its saying. I know that, when you repent and accept Christ, you are supposed to treat your past sins just as He does – forgiven and forgotten. I truly did that then I got saved, but the shadows of my past try to creep back into the quiet corners of my life every day. So many people killed. So many lives torn apart. So much precious time wasted. And all because of two arrogant men, me and McCoy, who would not turn away from violence.

My biggest mistake was to allow Uncle Jim Vance to get me worked up and angry about first one thing then another. He would relate to me some slur or slight that had come from the McCoy camp, and I would swell up like a bull-frog with my anger and then decide to take offense and then to be offensive. Yes, we wanted justice when Elliot was stabbed over in Pike County, but what we did to get it was not justified. Jim knew how to provoke me and took full advantage of that knowledge to get me to do things he wanted done. After I went off to war, he and what were then his Logan Wildcats preyed on both sides. It didn't matter whether your sympathies lay with the North or the South, you were fair game for them. They acted openly when attacking Yankee folks and secretly when attacking Confederate families. I am sure, but cannot prove, that he profited from the feud in some manner. He certainly did enough to keep it going. He has now answered to his eternal Judge, so I won't belabor the point.

In the same way, Ran'l McCoy allowed that slick lawyer, Perry Cline, to keep him hating us with a passion. Poor McCoy was a broken man, dead to anything but hate inside, after we burned his home and killed his children, it just took him some years to actually lie down and die. Cline was able to profit from all the fighting, just as much as Vance, if not more.

Either of us could have walked away during the course of the feud, but we both allowed pride and anger to provoke decisions that sent people to their deaths, both friend and foe. We Hatfields never intended to kill Alifair McCoy that night, it happened because we didn't do anything to prevent it. Poor old "Cotton" should never have been there that night, and especially should not have been left alone with a loaded weapon. He was a victim of my anger as much as Alifair. That's the curse of decisions made in anger. They are like big rocks chunked into a pond, creating ripples that extend far beyond where the rocks strike. Everywhere those ripples reach, they change a life, a situation, an event. Many times, the ripples provoke someone one on the other side to chunk a rock or two themselves, bringing new ripples back upon you. Let that happen enough times, and you find that the pond is full of rocks and the waves have washed you all away.

Son, I know we've talked about this subject before and that you were somewhat close to Uncle Jim. I'm not blaming him. I'm blaming myself. I made decisions in anger that could not be taken back. Jim did nothing that I did not allow, even condone, in my pride. I think about these things daily, and will until the Lord calls me home. My sins are covered by Jesus' Blood, but their fruit is ever with me. Who knows what kind of life there might have been for Levicy, me and you kids if I had been able to bridle my passions? Too late now______________________

Boys : I found your Daddy sitting by the fire with this letter in his hands. I won't add to it, but do implore you to take it to heart in all of your dealings and to teach it to your children. If you do, it will be a blessing to your family for generations to come. I've sent for Doc Chafin, who can't have gotten very far since lunch-time, and will send a messenger to you as well bearing this letter. Do you come to us as quickly as you can to help make the arrangements for your father's burial. He wants to be on the hill up at Sary Ann. I guess that's a good enough place for me as well. See you soon.

Love from your Mother
Levicy Chafin Hatfield

BUSINESS PRINCIPLE : Decisions made in anger lead almost inevitably to trouble, be that broken relationships, financial loss, public embarrassment or even death. Countries have gone to war over foolish pride and anger. Businesses have been destroyed from within because an executive could not control temper and passion. Anger can be channeled into resolve and positive energy, or it can be allowed to poison relationships. It is up to you. Just keep in mind that your angry decision is likely to provoke other angry decisions that will not take you where you want to go. Like Devil Anse and Ran'l McCoy, you may see everything you hold dear go up in smoke when the fire of your anger is allowed to burn unchecked.

HISTORICAL NOTE : The following is a brief chronology of the Hatfield-McCoy Feud, which was a very real and very violent event. Most of the deaths came as people were gunned down from ambush, with only one pitched battle.

YEAR	EVENT
1863	Logan Wildcats formed by Devil Anse Hatfield, later led by Jim Vance
1865	Civil War ends; Asa Harmon McCoy (Yankee) is killed near home. No prosecution resulted.
1878	Ran'l McCoy accuses Floyd Hatfield of stealing a pig but loses in a jury trial when Bill Staton, a McCoy neighbor, lies for Hatfield.
1880	Bill Staton murdered by Paris and Sam McCoy. Sam is tried and acquitted. Johnse Hatfield brings Roseanne McCoy home with him.
1881	Pregnant Roseanne returns to her aunt in KY. Her brothers catch Johnse over there and intend to kill him. Roseanne rides to get Devil Anse, who saves his son. Roseanne catches measles and miscarries, moves to Pikeville. Johnse marries Nancy McCoy, daughter of Asa (deceased).
1882	Elliot Hatfield killed on election day by Bud, Tolbert and Pharmer McCoy. Devil Anse and his followers take the three into custody and execute them on the banks of the Tug Fork of the Big Sandy River. Later, Jeff McCoy is killed on the banks of the Tug.
1887	The governor of Kentucky appoints "Bad" Frank Phillips to capture the murderers of the three McCoy brothers (1882), with little regard for extradition laws.

YEAR	EVENT
1888	The Hatfields respond to pressure by burning the McCoy cabin in the early hours of New Year's Day, killing Alifair and Calvin McCoy. Their mother is driven to insanity by her grief. Roseanne dies in Pikeville.
1889	Hatfield clan members are arrested and tried for the 1888 murders.
1890	Ellison "Cotton" Mounts, a Hatfield clan member with learning disabilities, is executed for killing Alifair McCoy. Other clan members are imprisoned, with Anse's brother, Wall, dying in jail.
1891	The feud ends.

The Hatfield Clan is pictured on the following page. Vicie Chafin Hatfield is sitting to the right of her husband, Devil Anse, at left. She is my grandfather's aunt. The blond boy to the right, with the pistol, is my great-uncle, Tom Chafin.

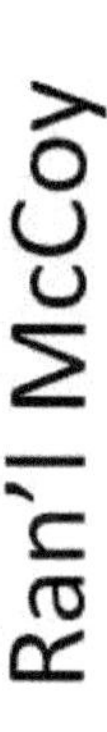

Ran'l McCoy

Devil Anse Hatfield

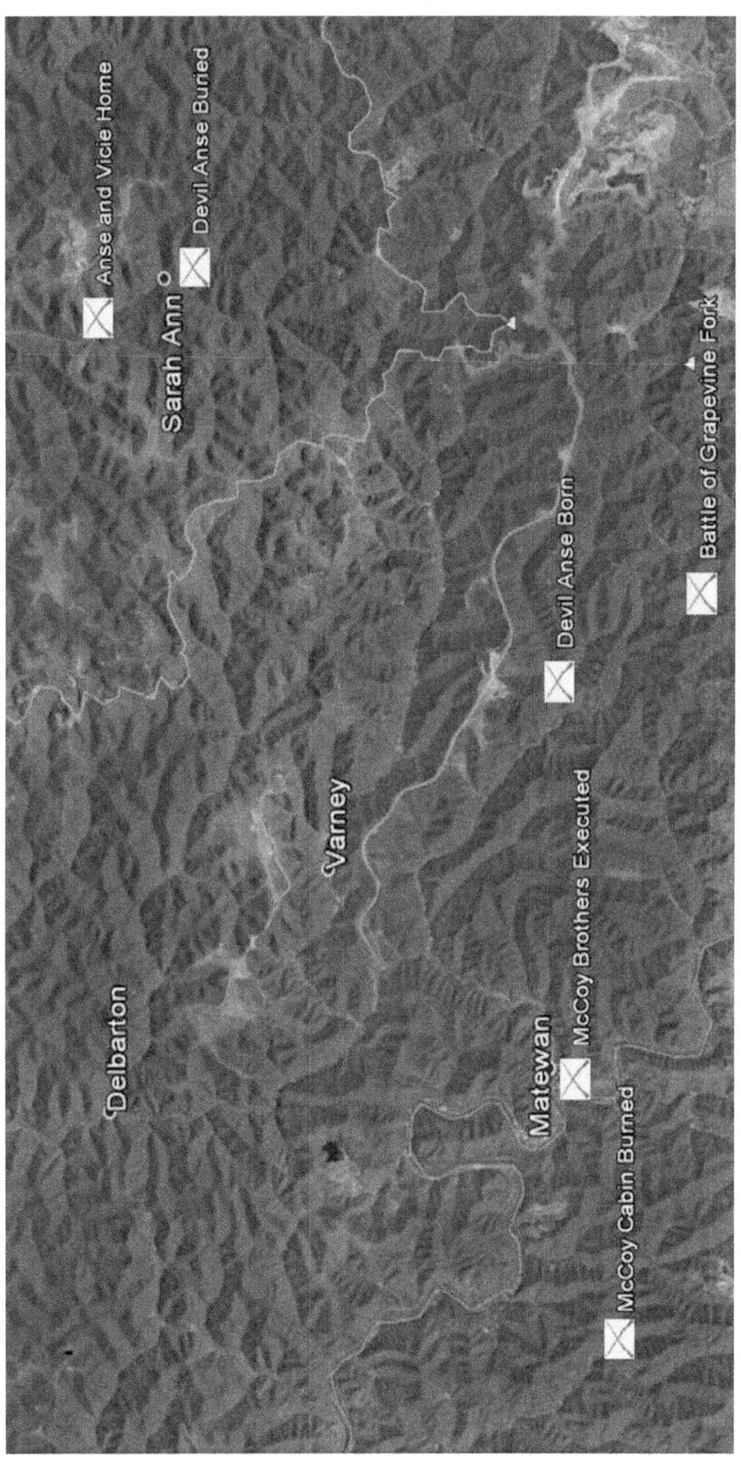

BIRTHPLACE OF THE FEUD

www.ingramcontent.com/pod-product-compliance
Lightning Source LLC
Chambersburg PA
CBHW051821170526
45167CB00005B/2099

* 9 7 8 1 4 9 6 0 6 7 7 2 2 *